This Book Is Dedicated to the Memory of

_____

from

_____

I Remember You

A Grief Journal

I Remember You

A Grief Journal

Laynee Wild

HarperSanFrancisco
A Division of HarperCollins*Publishers*

Permissions/acknowledgments on page 164.

I REMEMBER YOU: A Grief Journal. Copyright © 1995 by Laynee Wild. All rights reserved. Printed in the United States of America. No part of this book may be used or reproduced in any manner whatsoever without written permission, except in the case of brief quotations embodied in critical articles and reviews. For information address HarperCollins Publishers, 10 East 53rd Street, New York, NY 10022.

Cover and interior design © Sharon Smith, 1994

Cover and interior photographs © David Wakely, 1994

FIRST EDITION

ISBN 0–06–251091–6 (cloth : acid-free paper)

95 96 97 98 99 ❖ RRD(C) 10 9 8 7 6 5 4 3 2 1

This edition is printed on acid-free paper that meets the American National Standards Institute Z39.48 Standard.

In Search of a Mustard Seed

A young woman was grieving uncontrollably over the death of her
beloved son, her firstborn child, who was only about a year old. She went
to the Buddha, laid the body of her child at his feet, and told him her story
in hopes of finding an antidote to her child's "malady" that would restore
him to consciousness. The Buddha, renowned for his miraculous healing
powers, listened with infinite compassion, then said gently, "Go down to
the city and bring me back a mustard seed. The mustard seed will provide
the proper antidote. But you must accept the mustard seed only from a
house in which there has never been a death."

The young woman set off immediately for the city. She stopped at the
first house she came to and said, "I have been told by the Buddha to ob-
tain a mustard seed from a house that has never been touched by death."

"We cannot oblige you, for this house has known countless deaths,"
was the response. She moved on to the next house. "Many people have
died in this house," they said. She continued on from house to house until
she had been to every household in the city. Finally she realized the
Buddha's condition could not be fulfilled.

She took the body of her child to the burning-ground and there sub-
mitted him to the fires of cremation. After saying good-bye for the last
time, she returned to the Buddha. "Did you bring the mustard seed?"
he asked.

Buddhist parable

This journal holds many possibilities. Within these pages, you can celebrate and commemorate the life of the person to whom this book is dedicated. This can be a place to gently explore the emotions, thoughts, and dreams that emerge as you move through this major transition in your life. Here you can address any unfinished business in your relationship with the one you are remembering, so that you can gain new perspectives and inner peace. In this book, you can note your reflections on life and death, on faith and hope; you can dwell with whatever is on your mind and in your heart.

I am a counselor by profession and have walked with many individuals and families on their paths through grief. But it wasn't until my mother died that I truly began to grasp grief's profound complexity. Journaling has been an essential instrument of recovery, helping me stay grounded through the torrents of thoughts and feelings. Using a specially designated grief journal has further helped me reach a certain peace of mind and heart, because I know my memories and experiences are safely stored in a specific, comforting home all their own.

This journal can be a home for your experiences. As you tell your story, your words will lead you on your own unique, personal passage through the healing process of grief. As you give life to these pages, you will also be breathing life into your relationship with the one who has passed on.

Joseph Campbell said, "It is by going down into the abyss that we recover the treasures of life." May this book be a comforting companion on your journey.

To suppress the grief, the pain, is to condemn oneself to a living death. Living fully means *feeling* fully; it means becoming completely one with what you are experiencing and not holding it at arm's length.

Philip Kapleau
The Wheel of Life and Death

A Few Words About Grief

When someone close to us dies, we embark on a journey, a journey not of our choosing and with no precise course. It can be a time of mental and emotional confusion, and with the confusion comes the feeling of power-lessness. Many of us react to this powerlessness by seeking to gain some control, some answers. We want to know how and why this happened; we want to know what we can expect to happen next.

At a time when we're seeking answers, we're left instead with a grief process that is unpredictable and unstructured. There are no concrete, linear stages; there is no predetermined time line. There are several layers of grief that occur simultaneously: grief for what is no more, grief for what never was, grief for what will never be. And other losses — both past and anticipated — may push their way in and demand the heart's attention as well.

Whether the relationship with the one who has died was completely sat-isfying or was troubled by unresolved issues, each of us will probably have a wide array of thoughts and feelings associated with grief. Sometimes the expression of these feelings may seem irrational; for in-stance, bursting into a fit of laughter when only moments before you were sobbing. Sometimes several conflicting emotions may be present at the same time: One of my clients felt anger, sadness, and even happiness—simultaneously—when her father died after a lengthy and painful battle with AIDS. And sometimes you may not feel anything at all. The most important thing to remember throughout the process is that *no matter what thoughts or feelings surface, let them be present without judgment.* Stay with them for a while, and trust that they are there for a reason. The more we try to judge, rationalize, or hurry the grief process, the more we get in the way of our own healing.

Of course, there isn't one time limit for everyone's grieving and healing process, but a minimum of one year is generally the *starting* point. The year following the death will be one of "firsts" to experience apart from the one who has died. There will be the first of every holiday that had traditionally been celebrated together: the first birthday, both our own and that of the one we mourn; the first anniversary—of marriage, of death, of any other significant date; and so on. Each of these is likely to evoke a whole new wave of thoughts, feelings, and memories. We must give ourselves the time and space we need to ride each wave out gently.

I myself have often longed for some structure and theory that would
compartmentalize and chart my pain. But, there is no single story
or timetable or passageway through the sorrow.

Helen Vozenilek
Loss of the Ground-Note

Common Emotional Experiences

Discussed below are a number of emotions common to grief. Through
journaling, these experiences and feelings can be explored and better un-
derstood. (If you would like a more detailed description of these emotions, there is a list of suggested readings at the back of this journal.)

•**Denial.** Denial is, I believe, one of the oddest emotions of all. It's the "I
just don't believe she (or he) is gone" feeling that lives within the rational
mind, which is fully aware of the facts. Denial often takes us by surprise.
The phone rings and for a split second we think that it might be the one
person it can't be. Then, within the very same second, reality hits —
usually right in the stomach.

•**Numbness.** A feeling often associated with denial is numbness. For some
of us, this sensation is similar to how it must feel to walk around in an insu-
lated bubble, separated from both the outside world and our own feelings.
Depending on how traumatic the death was and how many responsibilities
we must attend to immediately following it, we can go numb for days,
months, or even years. Then, once our responsibilities and other distrac-
tions diminish, we thaw and start to feel. And the rule is that *we must feel in
order to heal.* As difficult and as frightening as this may be, remember the
wisdom of Robert Frost: "The best way out is always through."

•**Anger.** Anger is a natural emotional response to how powerless we feel when someone we care about dies. Sometimes our anger is directed outward, at doctors, clergy, God, family, or friends. Sometimes it's directed inward, at ourselves. Sometimes it has no clear direction whatsoever, and we find ourselves just plain irritable. And sometimes it's directed at the one who has died. We need to give ourselves permission to have our anger without shame or guilt because anger, too, is a necessary part of healing.

•**Regret.** When death arrives, we are frequently catapulted into a deep examination of the relationship's entire history as well as the events leading up to the actual death. The *if onlys, what ifs,* and *could haves* are the instruments we use for dissection, as though we're obsessed with trying to redo or undo history. When the *could haves* become *should haves,* guilt often becomes associated with regret. Avoid using the word *should.* It is too often used to punish yourself, when what you really need is to take care of yourself.

The challenge is to allow these thoughts and feelings to come, *but not to get attached to them.* Just notice them and write about them; they will pass, and each day will bring you closer to acceptance.

•**Sadness.** The sadness and depression that are a natural part of the grieving process often come in waves. Yet the waves are not always accompanied by tears. Instead, we may find ourselves feeling more like spectators of than participants in life, lacking interest or pleasure in activities that we once heartily enjoyed. We may become unable to concentrate, and there may be changes in our eating and sleeping behaviors. Some people think about suicide, because joining the one who has died may seem more inviting than dealing with life and the pain of grief.

Thoughts like these are natural, but if they persist it would be wise to seek help from a professional counselor.

Though our tendency may be to isolate ourselves, it's important that, instead, we surround ourselves with loving people who can provide the necessary emotional support. Often, these people have had a significant loss themselves, and through the pain of loss comes a unique kind of wisdom and understanding.

•**Acceptance.** We are in a state of acceptance when we no longer feel compelled to redo or undo the past. We can face death and release our loved one so that we can both move on. We are free to live in the present again, equipped with new understanding, enlightenment.

Acceptance may last only moments before a new wave of emotion carries us back out to sea. In time, we may dwell almost continuously in this quiet place of resolution, with only an occasional wave. It is crucial that we not resist the tides but instead give in to them, and trust that after each wave we will be brought safely back to shore.

> Should you shield the canyon from the windstorms
> you would never see the beauty of their carvings.

Elisabeth Kübler-Ross

Journaling Suggestions

There is no "right" way to keep a journal. Give yourself permission to write whatever your heart tells you. Allow yourself to be free and imaginative. Write poetry. Write a eulogy. Write prayers. Construct imaginary dialogues with the one who has passed on. Transcribe song lyrics that particularly speak to you, or compose your own songs. Use colored pens and illustrate the pages. Cut out and paste in an article or image that comforts you; slip a treasured photo or letter between the pages; press a leaf you found on the first day you smiled again. There are unlimited ways to communicate with yourself and with the spirit of the one who has died. Explore them all.

Here are some specific suggestions to help you get started.

STORE PRECIOUS MEMORIES

> Try to strike that delicate balance
> between a yesterday that should
> be remembered
> and a tomorrow that must be created.

Earl A. Grollman
Living When a Loved One Has Died

After my mom died, I wrote a detailed story of my last days with her. Death was such an awe-inspiring and powerful experience that I knew I had to preserve my perceptions of it as completely as possible. I encourage you to do the same.

Where were you when your loved one died? What were your initial feelings? What happened next? What were the last words that passed between you? Was there a funeral or memorial service, and what was it like? What else is important for you to remember about this profound, life-changing event?

Throughout the days, weeks, and years ahead, you can expect all kinds of memories to surface. Some may be welcome and pleasant; others may be filled with pain and regret. Write about them all, because together they weave the genuine and complex tapestry of your history with the one who has passed on.

COMMUNICATE THROUGH LETTERS

> That which must be said and isn't will repeat itself, again and again,
> until, in some way, it finds its home.
>
> **Stephanie Ericsson**
> *Companion Through the Darkness*

Your loved one may be gone but the relationship lives on. Through letter-writing, you can breathe new life into that relationship and continue to strengthen it.

To begin, you might just write letters about your day-to-day thoughts and feelings. Write about significant events, about thoughts and feelings that are evoked during each anniversary or holiday. Tell how it felt when you had dinner at what used to be her or his favorite restaurant, or when you heard that old song on the radio that always brought back special memories for the two of you. Whenever you feel the urge to call her or him, sit down and write instead. It may take practice before you are comfortable communicating this way. Be patient with yourself and with the process.

What went unsaid? What is left to say? Say it now. All of it. I learned much from my mom's death, and I longed to share what I learned with her. I learned what it was like to lose a mother to cancer. My mom had never quite recovered from the loss of her mother—who died of cancer before I was born—and she would often express feelings that I could never really understand. Until she, too, died. Clients and friends have shared with me various concerns, some of which matched my own: Did I say "I love you" enough? Did I tell her how much I appreciated her? Even if we did express these feelings, our concern probably means we need to say it some more. It's never too late.

It's not uncommon to go through periods of regression, to slip into a prior stage of emotional development or to feel like a child again. At times, I felt homesick and needed "Daddy" nearby—emotions that I initially found to be rather embarrassing until I was able to release judgment. It's essential to listen to the child within, to respect the crucial needs of attention and nurturing. Writing with the hand we don't usually write with can be a particularly useful technique at these times. While it may sound peculiar, it sometimes helps us get more closely in touch with our inner child and better able to express the feelings and thoughts that occur at that primitive level.

As mentioned above, it is natural to respond to death with anger, regret, guilt, and other uncomfortable emotions. These feelings can be especially difficult to cope with when we have unresolved conflicts with the deceased. When the emotions are externalized, they can be worked through effectively and released, freeing us from the negativity of the past and allowing us to live more fully in the present.

Writing letters about each piece of "unfinished business" is a good method of helping this working-through process. Write about these issues in paragraph form, or make lists of them. Try writing a separate letter for each cluster of emotions; this will allow you to work through them more thoroughly as they work through you. Here are some suggestions for beginning your sentences:

I resent . . .

I felt hurt when . . .

I regret . . .

If only . . .

I wish . . .

I'm sorry . . .

As you address each of these emotions in your letters, visualize the person you're writing to hearing and acknowledging your feelings. Imagine that this person can truly understand all that your heart is communicating, now that she or he is more directly linked with the higher powers of the universe. The ultimate goal is to achieve forgiveness—of the past, of the other, and of yourself.

RECORD VALUABLE DREAMS

> People come and go in life, but they never leave your dreams.
> Once they're in your subconscious, they are immortal.

Patricia Hampl

Keep this journal by your bed—one of its most valuable uses will be as a storehouse for precious dreams of the one you grieve. It is in our dreams that we have the unique opportunity to encounter the departed as if they were still alive in physical form—we can look at them, converse with them, even touch them. And much of our healing from grief is achieved through our dreams because, in them, our emotions are raw and unfiltered, without the controls we put on them in the waking world.

Early in the grief process, it is common to have dreams that are disturbing reenactments of the initial trauma of the death. If these dreams recur, it might be a sign that we are stuck in denial. These repetitive dreams challenge us to confront reality. The more nightmarish the dreams, the louder the call to face what has happened and move on to the process of letting go. Although taking that next step may in itself seem frightening or unpleasant, the fact that we're having these dreams means we're ready to do so. Our dreaming self will guide us to where we need to go only when we're mentally and emotionally capable of being there.

While it may not be logical to be angry at someone for dying when it wasn't that person's choice, it is natural. In our dreams we can work through this anger. A young man shared one of his dreams with me, in which he and his recently deceased wife were at a party together. In the dream, his wife decided to leave early, and he was furious with her for doing so. The dream was a metaphor, because the young man was angry about her dying ("leaving early") when they had three young children to raise. His conscious self found it too disconcerting to have such irrational anger, so his dreaming self stepped in and provided an outlet for this repressed but natural emotion.

Another healing aspect of dreams is that they let us live out our *what ifs* and *if onlys*. We can become obsessive about these thoughts as we try to redo or undo some aspect of the past. Often, when the fantasy is played out in a dream, the urgency subsides. For example, I had a dream several weeks after my mom had passed on. In the dream she and I were together, and I had a certain awareness that she had only a week to live. I held her hand and promised her, through my tears, that I wouldn't leave her side all week. While I wrote down this dream, it occurred to me that this was, in fact, one of my greatest regrets: Although I was with her the night she died, I hadn't been with her during the week prior to her death. Instead of heeding the intuitive voice that told me to stay, I returned home on Monday, only to receive word on Tuesday that she was back in the hospital and in critical condition. By the time I arrived on Thursday, she was no longer able to communicate. She died the following night.

Most dreams reflect what was on our minds and in our hearts the day or night before. This means we can have some control over what we dream—we can consciously invite the one we miss into a dream by intentionally keeping her or him in our thoughts and prayers when we go to sleep. As an example, I'd like to share the following sequence of dreams that I had the first week following my mom's death:

I am at a social gathering. I walk into the kitchen and Mom is there! I'm thrilled to see her, and begin to make my way through the crowd to get near her. As I approach her, my rational mind kicks in, and I have the thought that she cannot really be here because she is dead. A fleeting image of her in her coffin, then we're back in the kitchen. She slowly fades from view before I can reach her. I wake myself as I call out, "No! Don't go!"

When I woke from this dream I was already crying, and the tears continued to flow for a long while. The days-old scar felt ripped open again, the fresh wound of loss gaping. As I wrote the dream in my journal, I decided that I wanted to have the dream again, to see her again, and this next time I wouldn't make her disappear. Instead, I would take advantage of her seemingly physical presence and embrace her. I kept this request to my inner self foremost in my mind and heart each night when I went to bed. Just two nights later I got my wish.

I am at the door of Mom's bedroom. She is standing by the glass doors at the other end, the light in the room dimmed by the drawn curtains. She looks as she did only a week or two before she died. I can sense a part of myself say "Go to her," and I do. I reach out and hug her gently, lovingly.

The strong kinesthetic memory of our embrace lingered for a long time after I woke. And I uttered a prayer of thanksgiving for my wish come true.

In some dreams, the contact with the one who has died feels uncannily real. These visitations are very common but often spoken of only in private. If you've already had a dream like this, or if you do in the future, respect it for what it is. Don't torture your rational mind looking for explanations. Simply write out the dream in detail and honor the sacred gift that has been bestowed on you.

A change is taking place, some painful growth, as in a snake during the shedding of its skin. It is difficult to adjust because I do not know who is adjusting; I am no longer that old person and not yet the new.

Peter Matthiessen
The Snow Leopard

In Closing

What comes after death? What is my purpose in life? Who am I now, now that this person who was such an integral part of me is gone? Now more than ever you might be asking yourself profound questions about life and death. And your faith—in yourself, life, and God—may be challenged as never before.

Your mind and heart might seem as though they're being strained to maximum capacity. At times you may find yourself wondering if the pain will ever lessen. It will, with time. But as Earl Grollman said, "*You* must help time do its healing."

So be gentle with yourself. Treat yourself with the same kind of love, respect, and patience that you would offer to a friend, and listen to yourself. Then use this journal to write what you hear.

We Remember Them

In the rising of the sun and in its going down,
 we remember them.
In the blowing of the wind and in the chill of winter,
 we remember them.
In the opening of buds and in the rebirth of spring,
 we remember them.
In the blueness of the sky and in the warmth of summer,
 we remember them.
In the rustling of leaves and in the beauty of autumn,
 we remember them.
In the beginning of the year and when it ends,
 we remember them.
When we are weary and in need of strength,
 we remember them.
When we are lost and sick at heart,
 we remember them.
When we have joys we yearn to share,
 we remember them.
So long as we live, they too shall live,
 for they are now a part of us, as
 we remember them.

Jewish prayer

I Remember You

A Grief Journal

There is an uncertain territory
between night and day.
It is neither light nor shadow:
        it is time.
An hour, a precarious pause,
a darkening page,
a page where I write,
slowly, these words.

        The afternoon
is an ember burning itself out.
The day turns, dropping its leaves.
A dark river files
at the edges of things.

        Tranquil, persistent
it drags them along, I don't know
   where.
Reality drifts off.

        I write:
I talk to myself
        —I talk to you.

Octavio Paz
"Letter of Testimony"

The way I feel

is like a robin

Whose babes have flown

to come no more

Like a tall oak tree

alone and cryin'

When the birds have flown

And the nest is bare.

Gordon Lightfoot
"The Way I Feel"

As no love is the same, no loss is.

Alla Renée Bozarth
A Journey Through Grief

Death

disrupts

the balance.

Phyllis Davies
Grief: Climb Toward Understanding

My soul is a broken field
plowed by pain.

Sara Teasdale
"The Broken Field"

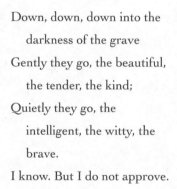

Down, down, down into the
    darkness of the grave
Gently they go, the beautiful,
    the tender, the kind;
Quietly they go, the
    intelligent, the witty, the
    brave.
I know. But I do not approve.
    And I am not resigned.

        Edna St. Vincent Millay
        "Dirge Without Music"

Loss is life's nonnegotiable side.

Stephanie Ericsson
Companion Through the Darkness

We have seen a fire of sticks

Burn out. The fire now

Burns in some other place. Where?

Who knows? These brands

Are burnt out.

Chuang Tzu
"Lau Tzu's Wake"

These days the silence is immense.
It is there deep down, not to be
  escaped.
The twittering flight of goldfinches,
The three crows cawing in the distance
Only brush the surface of this silence
Full of mourning, the long drawn-out
Tug and sigh of waters never still—
The ocean out there, and the inner
  ocean.

May Sarton
"The Silence Now"

It is crucial that we not resist the tides
but instead give in to them, and trust
that after each wave we will be
brought safely back to shore.

L. W.

Life must go on,

And the dead be forgotten;

Life must go on,

Though good men die;

Anne, eat your breakfast;

Dan, take your medicine;

Life must go on;

I forget just why.

Edna St. Vincent Millay
"Lament"

Death is a mirror in which the entire meaning
of life is reflected.

Sogyal Rinpoche
The Tibetan Book of Living and Dying

Sometimes it takes the knife that emotionally

pierces our heart, to pierce the walls that lie

in front of it.

Marianne Williamson
A Return to Love

Your pain is the breaking of the shell that encloses your understanding.
Even as the stone of the fruit must break, that its heart may stand in the sun, so must you know pain.
And could you keep your heart in wonder at the daily miracles of your life, your pain would not seem less wondrous than your joy;
And you would accept the seasons of your heart, even as you have always accepted the seasons that pass over your fields.
And you would watch with serenity through the winters of your grief.

Kahlil Gibran
The Prophet

The winter of first grief is a season of
hushed quiet, the soundlessness of new snow,
a numbness that has no voice to sing sorrow.

Mary Jane Moffat
In the Midst of Winter

Outlining the silence, my words
give shape to near-forgotten
memories. The silhouette of my
grief slowly begins to take form.

Sue Rochman
"Collecting Pieces"

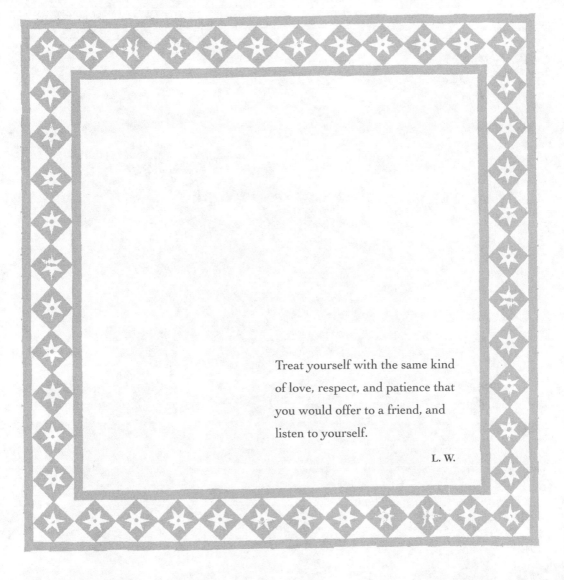

Treat yourself with the same kind
of love, respect, and patience that
you would offer to a friend, and
listen to yourself.

L. W.

Sometimes a weariness as heavy as the stone bridge spanning the banks hangs in my soul. Other times I am as numb as the morning fog that glances on the water's edge.

Helen Vozenilek
"Looking for My Mother"

There is no right response to death. You make it

up as you go along.

Joan Connor
"When Mountains Move"

Grieving is physical as well
as spiritual. It is an inner
journey, but its restlessness
demands movement.

Barbara Lazear Ascher
Landscape Without Gravity

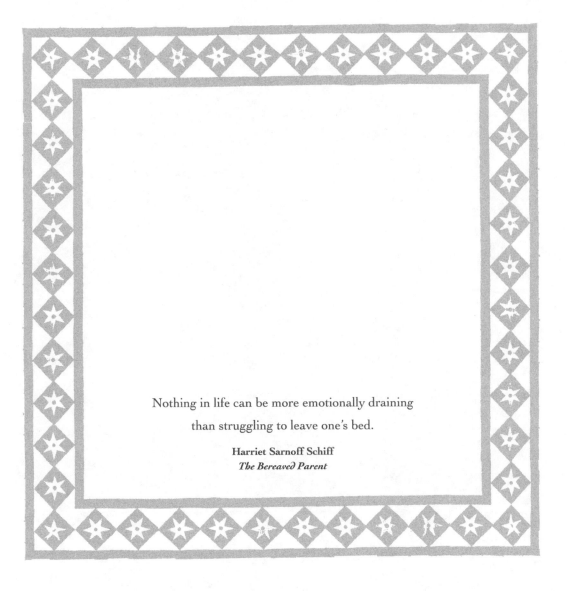

Nothing in life can be more emotionally draining

than struggling to leave one's bed.

Harriet Sarnoff Schiff
The Bereaved Parent

When pain and fatigue wrestle
fatigue wins. The eye shuts.
Then the pain rises again
    at dawn.
At first you can stare at it.
Then it blinds you.

Marge Piercy
"When a Friend Dies"

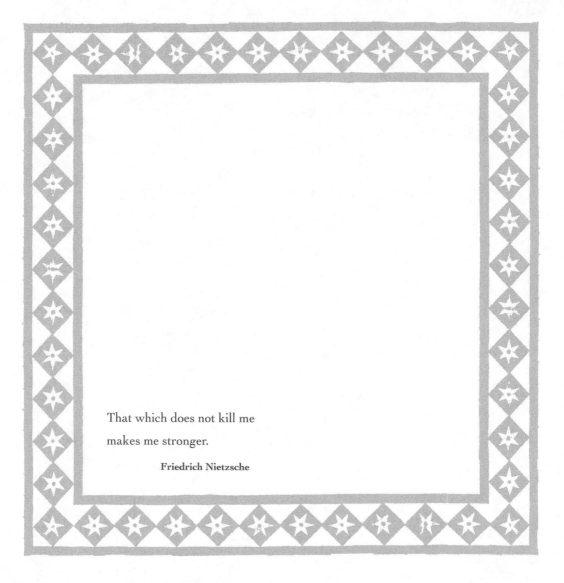

That which does not kill me

makes me stronger.

Friedrich Nietzsche

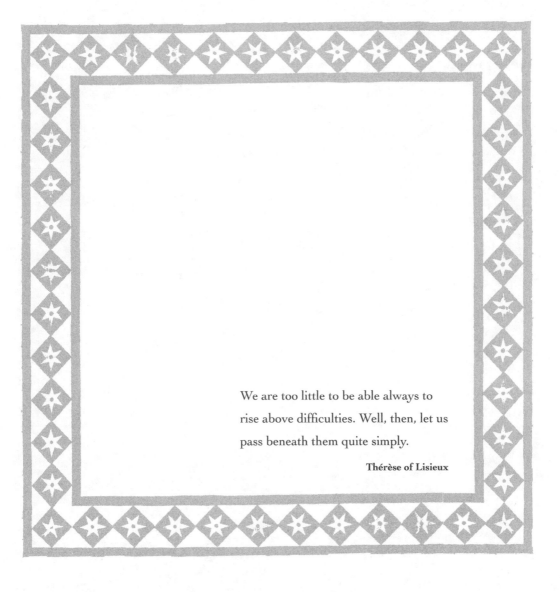

We are too little to be able always to
rise above difficulties. Well, then, let us
pass beneath them quite simply.

Thérèse of Lisieux

The sun, rising triumphant, tears himself from the
enveloping womb of the sea, and leaving behind
him the noonday zenith and all its glorious works,
sinks down again into the maternal depths, into
all-enfolding and all-regenerating night.

C. G. Jung

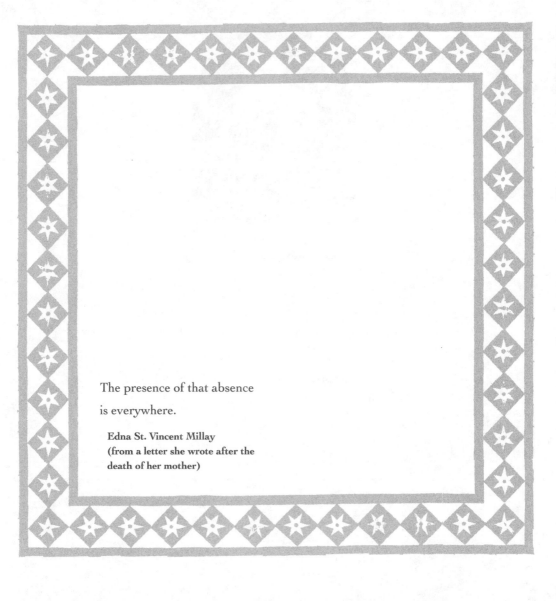

The presence of that absence
is everywhere.

**Edna St. Vincent Millay
(from a letter she wrote after the
death of her mother)**

Must we lose what we love
To know how much we loved it?

It is always there now,
That absence, that awful absence.

May Sarton
"Absence"

Food has no savor when we are starved for the
nourishment of our severed affections.

Mary Jane Moffat
In the Midst of Winter

This existence of ours is as transient as
    autumn clouds.
To watch the birth and death of beings is like
    looking at the movements of a dance.
A lifetime is like a flash of lightning in the sky,
Rushing by, like a torrent down a steep
    mountain.

Buddha

To be whole we must
deny nothing.

Stephen Levine
Who Dies?

The distance that the dead have gone

Does not at first appear—

Their coming back seems possible

For many an ardent year.

Emily Dickinson
Poems, Third Series (1896)

Mourning is the constant reawakening that
things are now different.

Stephanie Ericsson,
Companion Through the Darkness

Sorrow, like the river, must
be given vent lest it erode
its bank.

Earl A. Grollman
Living When a Loved One Has Died

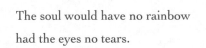

The soul would have no rainbow

had the eyes no tears.

John Vance Cheney

Grief is a wound that needs
attention in order to heal.

Judy Tatelbaum
The Courage to Grieve

In the country of pain we are each alone.

May Sarton
"The Country of Pain"

not knowing it would be the n

arted. I still regret lying down

by your side the whole night. Cou

t to you, touching you, have ease

fear or pain? I guess I'll never b

reams lately you've appeared yo

t's such a gift to experience ya

t reminds me of how you wer

so completely happy and joyf

ut the night we laughed so h

living room couch! That thing

on, but you just couldn't part

s so much relaxed joy among

embers there that night an

These notes are an umbilical cord. A way of
being with her still. Of bringing her close.
A release of a deep well of sorrow. Not a
work of imagination, with plot or argument,
but one of pain.

Toby Talbot
A Book About My Mother

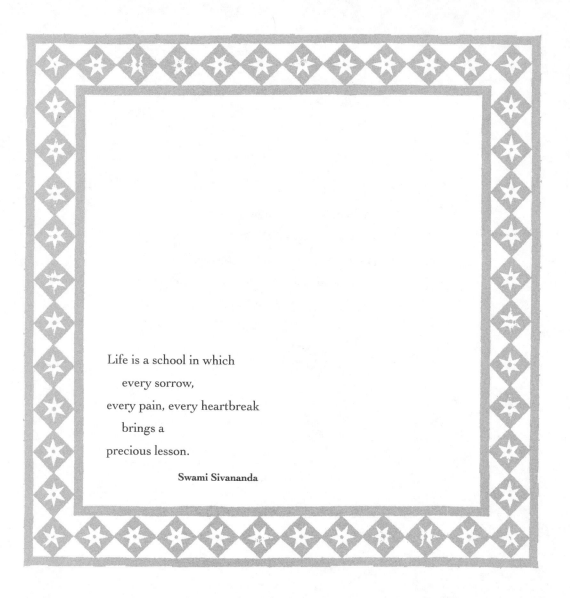

Life is a school in which
    every sorrow,
every pain, every heartbreak
    brings a
precious lesson.

Swami Sivananda

I walked a mile with Sorrow

And ne'er a word said she;

But, oh, the things I learned from her

When Sorrow walked with me.

Robert Browning

Some of you say, "Joy is greater than sorrow,"
and others say, "Nay, sorrow is the greater."
But I say unto you, they are inseparable.
Together they come, and when one sits alone
with you at your board, remember that the
other is asleep upon your bed.

Kahlil Gibran
The Prophet

Sometimes I go about pitying myself,

and all the time

I am being carried on great winds across the sky.

Ojibway
adapted by Robert Bly
from the translation of Frances Densmore

Memories

jolt me painfully,

then cradle me as I cry.

With passing time

tears are both

the dew of pain

and

pearls

of remembrance.

Phyllis Davies
Grief: Climb Toward Understanding

Will the circle be unbroken

by and by, Lord, by and by

There's a better home awaiting

in the sky, Lord, in the sky.

American folk song

Learning to live is learning to let go.

Sogyal Rinpoche
The Tibetan Book of Living and Dying

Tomorrow or the next life—
which comes first, we never
know.

Tibetan saying

Our question will not be Job's question "God, why are You doing this to me?" but rather "God, see what is happening to me. Can You help me?"

Harold S. Kushner
When Bad Things Happen to Good People

Unanswered why's are part of life.

Earl A. Grollman
Living When a Loved One Has Died

Go to the truth
beyond the mind.
Love is the bridge.

Stephen Levine
Who Dies?

The lights of things have turned on
more intensely just now as yours
has clicked immaculately off.

Patricia Hampl
"Last Letter"

Your body has its own
healing wisdom within it—
and so does your soul, the
expressive container of
your emotional life.

Alla Renée Bozarth
A Journey Through Grief

Strange—all that was is now magnified and monumental. At the same time, all that was now isn't.

Stephanie Ericsson
Companion Through the Darkness

nce of your fear or pain? I guess I'll neve

In my dreams lately you've appeared
d happy. It's such a gift to experience
ay again. It reminds me of how you u
y wedding, so completely happy and j
d how about the night we laughed so
out the old living room couch! That th
broken down, but you just couldn't par

There was so much relaxed joy amor
e family members there that night, a
u seemed to be having the most fun of
truly precious memory.

This Shabbat I lit candles and ble
ine and challah. I can truly appreciate
w important it was for you to have us
rry on tradition. How I wish I could
is newfound understanding with you.

A discarded dream is like gold

cast away.

Alexandra Kennedy
Losing a Parent

Death puts Life into perspective.

Ralph Waldo Emerson

Earth brings us into life

and nourishes us.

Earth takes us back again.

Birth and death are present in every moment.

Thich Nhat Hanh
"Gardening Gatha"

You are dipped up from the great
river of consciousness, and death
only pours you back.

Dorothy Canfield Fisher
The Bent Twig (1915)

Death is simply a shedding of the physical body

like the butterfly shedding its cocoon.

Elisabeth Kübler-Ross
On Life After Death

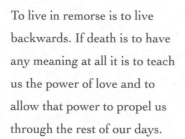

To live in remorse is to live
backwards. If death is to have
any meaning at all it is to teach
us the power of love and to
allow that power to propel us
through the rest of our days.

Barbara Lazear Ascher
Landscape Without Gravity

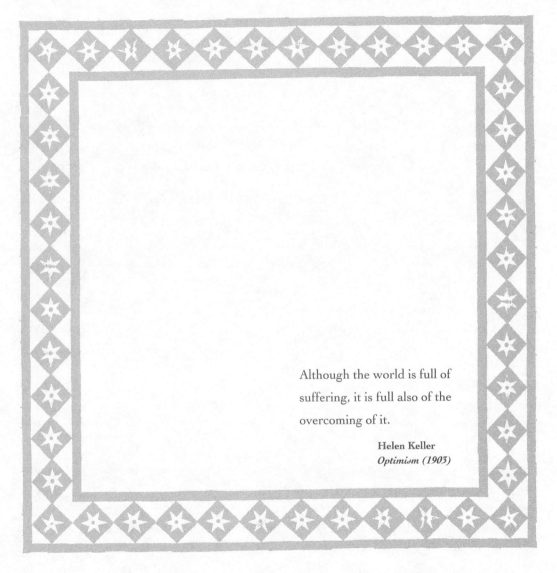

Although the world is full of
suffering, it is full also of the
overcoming of it.

Helen Keller
Optimism (1903)

Have patience with everything unresolved

in your heart

and try to love the questions themselves . . .

Don't search for the answers, which could not be

given to you now,

because you would not be able to live them.

And the point is, to live everything.

Live the questions now.

Perhaps then, someday far in the future,

you will gradually, without even noticing it,

live your way into the answer.

Rainer Maria Rilke
Letters to a Young Poet

The pain has now dulled and partially healed.
But like arthritis on a rainy day, it returns to
remind me that the limb is missing.

Betty Taylor-Thompson
"My Right Arm"

I do not choose patience.

Patience chooses for me.

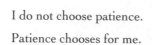

Stephanie Ericsson
Companion Through the Darkness

Without wishing it, we
human beings are placed
in situations in which
the great "principles"
entagle us in something,
and God leaves it to us to
find a way out.

C. G. Jung

Just as when the waves lash at the shore, the rocks suffer no damage but are sculpted and eroded into beautiful shapes, so our characters can be molded and our rough edges worn smooth by changes.

Sogyal Rinpoche
The Tibetan Book of Living and Dying

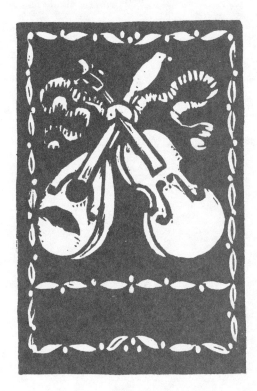

This world is not conclusion.

A sequel stands beyond—

Invisible, as Music—

But positive, as Sound.

Emily Dickinson
Poems, Third Series (1896)

All life, living or "dead," is interwoven like silk
threads in a fine brocade.

Philip Kapleau
The Wheel of Life and Death

Some days I can look at her photograph and the image revives her, reinforces her for me. On other days I gaze at her and am blinded with tears. Newly bereft.

Toby Talbot
A Book About My Mother

Rich tears! What power
lies in those falling drops.

Mary Delarivier Manley
The Royal Mischief (1696)

What wound did ever heal
but by degrees?

William Shakespeare

The only grief that does not end is grief that
has not been fully faced.

Judy Tatelbaum
The Courage to Grieve

Darkness makes us aware of the
stars,
And so when dark hours arise,
They may hold a bright and lovely
thing,
We might never have known
otherwise.

Peter A. Lea

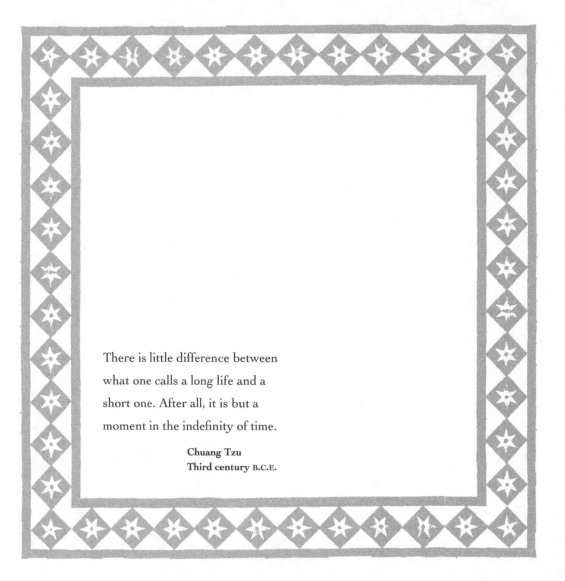

There is little difference between
what one calls a long life and a
short one. After all, it is but a
moment in the indefinity of time.

Chuang Tzu
Third century B.C.E.

She touches my memory
like she once touched
the keys of our old
upright piano.

Hermine Pinson
"Netta E."

So you mustn't be frightened . . .
if a sadness rises in front of you, larger
than any you have ever seen . . .
You must realize that something is
happening to you, that life has not
forgotten you, that it holds you in its
hand and will not let you fall.

Rainer Maria Rilke
Letters to a Young Poet

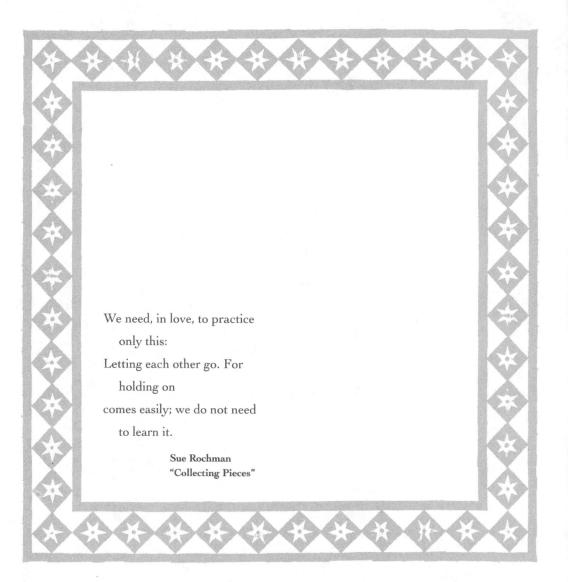

We need, in love, to practice
   only this:
Letting each other go. For
   holding on
comes easily; we do not need
   to learn it.

Sue Rochman
"Collecting Pieces"

It is in our dreams that we have the unique opportunity to encounter the departed as if they were still alive in physical form—we can look at them, converse with them, even touch them.

L. W.

Green leaves

That dawn after dawn

Grow yellow;

Red cheeks

That fade

With the passing days —

If our world

Is made up

Of such changes

As these,

Is it strange

That my heart

Is so sad?

Hsiao Kang
"Change"

It was nothing, just the present moment occurring for the first time in months.

Patricia Hampl
"The Moment"

Piece by piece, I reenter the world.
A new phase. A new body, a new
voice. Birds console me by flying,
trees by growing, dogs by the
warm patch they leave on the sofa
. . . It's like a slow recovery from a
sickness, this recovery of one's self.

Toby Talbot
A Book About My Mother

Grief is like a long valley, a winding valley where any bend may reveal a totally new landscape.

C. S. Lewis
A Grief Observed

Food—

the kitchen,

the store,

the dining table—

is where grief still confronts me.

Phyllis Davies
Grief: Climb Toward Understanding

Acceptance.

I finally reach it.

But something is wrong.

Grief is a circular staircase.

I have lost you.

      Linda Pastan
      "The Five Stages of Grief"

The only way to survive
bereavement is to step away
from it occasionally!

Harriet Sarnoff Schiff
The Bereaved Parent

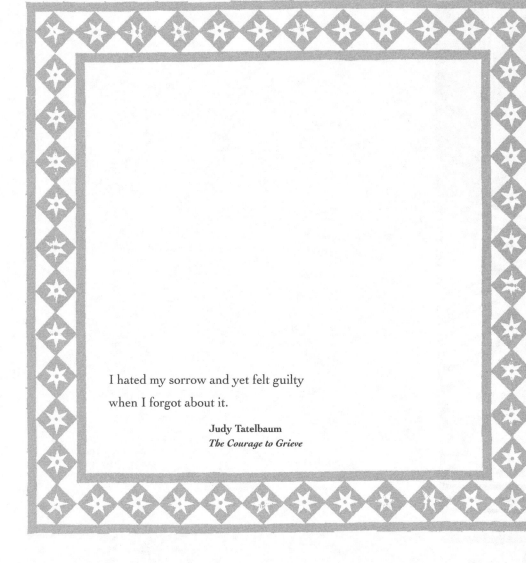

I hated my sorrow and yet felt guilty
when I forgot about it.

Judy Tatelbaum
The Courage to Grieve

No matter what thoughts or
feelings surface, let them be
present without judgment.

L. W.

We do best homage to our dead by living our lives fully even in the shadow of our loss.

Jewish prayer

Sometimes I feel loyalty means having the things she always wanted and never had. But when I am happy, I feel I am being disloyal by having more than she had.

Bookda Gheisar
"An Unfinished Story"

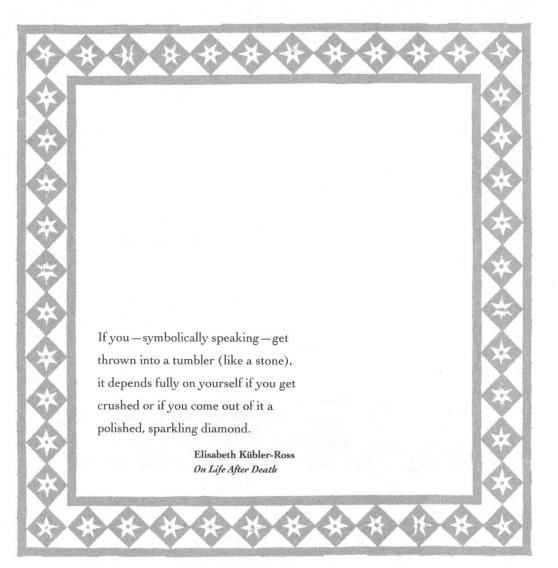

If you—symbolically speaking—get
thrown into a tumbler (like a stone),
it depends fully on yourself if you get
crushed or if you come out of it a
polished, sparkling diamond.

Elisabeth Kübler-Ross
On Life After Death

You cannot prevent the birds of sorrow
from flying over your head,
but you can prevent them from building
nests in your hair.

Chinese proverb

I have been trying to
make the best of grief
and am just beginning
to learn to allow it to
make the best of me.

Barbara Lazear Ascher
Landscape Without Gravity

The lowest ebb is the turn
of the tide.

Henry Wadsworth Longfellow

Even a seed must experience its own version of pain as it pushes through dark soil and cracks open its outer husk, to emerge in a burst of green growth into a vast new world of warm sunlight.

Alexandra Kennedy
Losing a Parent

In her loss I am almost bankrupt,
and my life is a bitterness, but I
am content: for she has been
enriched with that most precious
of all gifts — that gift which makes
all other gifts mean and poor —
death.

Mark Twain
(after his daughter Jean's death)

There will always be a hole that will
never be filled but it doesn't mean
that I feel so empty anymore.

Karen Kandik
"Finding Home"

Birth is a beginning,
And death a destination;
But life is a journey,
A sacred pilgrimage
Made stage by stage—
From birth to death
To life everlasting.

Alvin Fine

Every arrival foretells a leave-taking: every birth
a death. Yet each death and departure comes to
us as a surprise, a sorrow never anticipated. Life
is a long series of farewells; only the
circumstances should surprise us.

Jessamyn West
The Life I Really Lived

The game is never over

Birth and death are even

The terms are not final.

Chuang Tzu
"Autumn Floods"

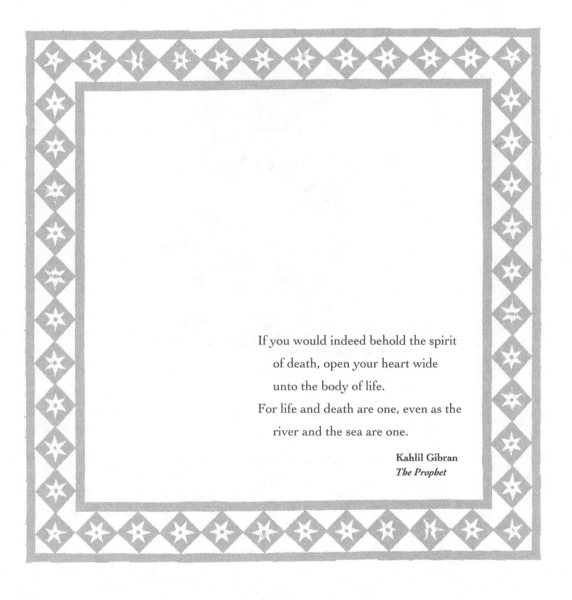

If you would indeed behold the spirit

of death, open your heart wide

unto the body of life.

For life and death are one, even as the

river and the sea are one.

Kahlil Gibran
The Prophet

Wherever death is commemorated,

I commemorate;

Wherever prayers are prayed, I pray.

Daisy Aldan
"Is It the Time of the Clock Without Hands?"

Tears may be dried up,

but the heart —

never.

Marguerite de Valois (1553–1615)
French princess and scholar

I didn't keep the ashes. I let them go, all of them, and I thought this is the most you can love somebody. . . . Now I want to love living people that way too. With mostness. With releasing.

Mary Jane Westbrook
"Unconscious Gifts"

Just as whole forests burn to the ground and
eventually grow anew, just as spring follows
winter, so it is nature's way that through it all,
whatever we suffer, we can keep on growing.

Judy Tatelbaum
The Courage to Grieve

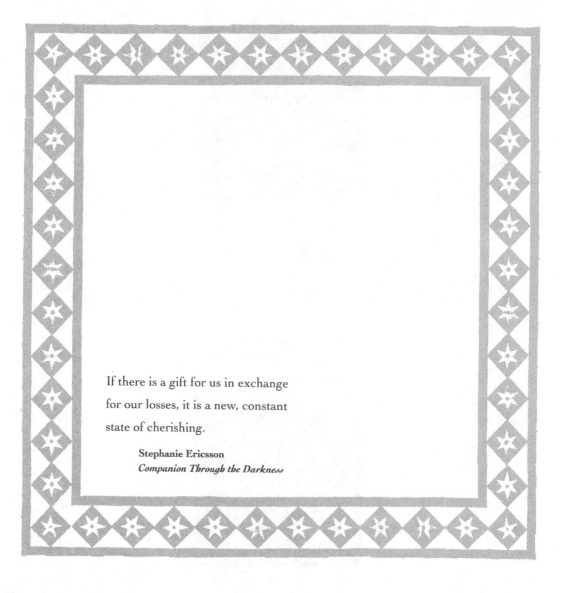

If there is a gift for us in exchange
for our losses, it is a new, constant
state of cherishing.

Stephanie Ericsson
Companion Through the Darkness

There is a rent, a tear, a rip in the
fabric of my life that can't ever be
completely sewn up or patched
over, but which lets in both the
darkness that is the underworld
and a world of astonishing—the
only word which can describe it
is celestial—light.

Alison Townsend
"Small Comforts"

Certain smells, certain moments when I feel
unloved, certain aspects of the Christmas rituals,
and hundreds of other ordinary details of life, will
reopen the wound. But at least now I can let it
bleed for a while and go on. At least now I can be
open, not only to those painful moments, but also
to the many joys of my life.

Judith Barrington
"Grief Postponed"

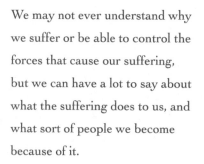

We may not ever understand why
we suffer or be able to control the
forces that cause our suffering,
but we can have a lot to say about
what the suffering does to us, and
what sort of people we become
because of it.

Harold S. Kushner
When Bad Things Happen to Good People

I am one with all those who have
ever suffered pain. I am learning
something new — that it is
necessary to be grateful for pain
in order to learn anything from it.

Arupa Chiarini
"The Edith Papers"

These things are beautiful beyond belief:
    The pleasant weakness that comes after pain,
    The radiant greenness that comes after rain,
    The deepened faith that follows after grief,
    And the awakening to love again.

Author unknown

I still miss those I loved who are no longer
with me but I find I am grateful for having
loved them. The gratitude has finally conquered
the loss.

Rita Mae Brown
Starting from Scratch

Memory can tell us only what we were, in
company with those we loved; it cannot help
us find what each of us, alone, must now
become. Yet no person is really alone; those
who live no more echo still within our
thoughts and words, and what they did has
become woven into what we are.

Jewish prayer

Suggested Readings

Ascher, Barbara Lazear. *Landscape Without Gravity: A Memoir of Grief.* New York: Delphinium Books, Inc., 1992. The moving story of the author's personal grief process surrounding her brother's death from AIDS.

Davies, Phyllis. *Grief: Climb Toward Understanding.* New York: Carol Communications, 1988. Poetry inspired by the author's loss of her teenage son in a plane crash. Also includes a valuable resource guide.

Ericsson, Stephanie. *Companion Through the Darkness: Inner Dialogues on Grief.* New York: HarperCollins Publishers, Inc., 1993. Intensely honest journal entries and personal reflections about grief and recovery, written by a woman who was pregnant at the time of her husband's sudden death.

Grollman, Earl A. *Living When a Loved One Has Died.* Boston: Beacon Press, 1977. A widely recommended, heartfelt, and easy-to-read treasure.

Kübler-Ross, Elisabeth. *On Life After Death.* Berkeley: Celestial Arts, 1991. Inspirational reading by one of the most widely acclaimed experts on death.

Kushner, Harold S. *When Bad Things Happen to Good People.* New York: Avon Books, 1981. Challenged by the death of his young son, a rabbi sensitively addresses the question of how to have faith in God when life seems unfair.

Moffat, Mary Jane, ed. *In the Midst of Winter.* New York: Random House, Inc., 1982. An excellent compilation of grief-related poetry, prose, and short stories.

O'Toole, Donna. *Aarvy Aardvark Finds Hope.* North Carolina: Mountain Rainbow Publications, 1988. A marvelous, illustrated storybook about loss, grief, hope, and friendship, for both adults and children.

Vozenilek, Helen, ed. *Loss of the Ground-Note: Women Writing About the Loss of Their Mothers.* Los Angeles: Clothespin Fever Press, 1992. This collection of short essays is a must for all women grieving the loss of their mothers.